UNB

THE LIFE AND TIME OF LISA MARIE PRESLEY

Loretta Davies

Table of content

Introduction

"Unbreakable: The Life and Times of Lisa Marie Presley" is a captivating excursion into the surprising presence of an up in the lady shadow of a legend that arose as her own exceptional power. In this essential record, we sojourn into the promising and less encouraging times, the victories and inconveniences, and the extreme soul that portrays Lisa Marie Presley.

Ordinarily familiar with the amazing Presley custom, Lisa Marie's life will without a doubt be everything beside common. She conveyed the significance of her father's legacy as the famous Elvis Presley's daughter while delivering her own distinct style in the music industry, to say the least. In any case, behind the essential façade, Lisa Marie's cycle was one of self-exposure, individual battles, and dedicated assertion.

In "UNBREAKABLE," we examine the enormous influence that Lisa Marie's father had on her life and the decisions she made to spread out her own personality by stripping back the layers of her stunning persona. We loosen the web of her life, revealing the flaws, strength, and adaptability that have characterized her journey, from her underlying seemingly forever at the center of consideration regarding her chart-topping music job to the storm feelings and heartbreaks.

Through five star social events, agreeable snippets of data, and requesting examination, we welcome you to see the untold stories, the confidential minutes, and the courageous soul of a world lady with a consistent spin. We research her occupation as the guardian of the Elvis Presley inheritance, her energized obligation to saving her dad's memory, and the difficulties she experienced on the way.

"UNBREAKABLE" offers an immense and close assessment of an everyday presence stayed in the glare of the public eye, where achievement and evaluation strolled indivisible. It welcomes you to comprehend the lady behind the name, the young woman who respected her dad's inheritance while shaping her own very solid flaw on the world.

Join Loretta Davies as she embarks on a journey through triumphs and tragedies, love and hardship, and the steadfast spirit that has portrayed Lisa Marie Presley's life and times. This is her story, one of perseverance, adaptability, and a constant determination to discover her own voice in the midst of the important resonances.

CHAPTER 1. EARLY LIFE AND FAMILY BACKGROUND OF LISA MARIE PRESLEY

Lisa Marie Presley, born on February 1, 1968, in Memphis, Tennessee, is the only child of the famous rock and roll legend Elvis Presley and his beautiful wife Priscilla Presley. Lisa Marie's early life was marked by a unique blend of privilege, fame, and tragedy.

Growing up, Lisa Marie was exposed to the world of music and showbiz from a very young age, she had a golden yet gilded childhood, her father gave her all she ever wanted, she was lavished with gifts and many impromptu concert, because Her father, Elvis Presley, was one of the most influential and celebrated musicians of the 20th century. However, Lisa Marie's early years were also overshadowed by her parents' highly publicized divorce in 1973, when she was just five years old.

Despite the separation, both Elvis and Priscilla remained devoted parents to Lisa Marie.

Following her parents' divorce, Lisa Marie split her time between living with her mother in Beverly Hills and spending vacations at her father's Graceland mansion in Memphis. These contrasting environments exposed her to different lifestyles and helped shape her understanding of fame, family, and her own identity.

Tragedy struck the Presley family in August 1977 when Lisa Marie was just nine years old. Her father, Elvis Presley, passed away suddenly, leaving a significant void in her life. This loss had a profound impact on Lisa Marie, who would later inherit her father's estate and carry on his musical legacy.

As Lisa Marie grew older, she developed a strong passion for music and sought to carve her own path in the industry. She signed a recording contract in 1997 and released her debut album, "To Whom It May Concern," which garnered moderate success. Over the years, she has released several albums, exploring various musical styles and genres.

In terms of family relationships, Lisa Marie has been married multiple times. Her first marriage was to musician Danny Keough in 1988, and they had two children together: a daughter named Danielle Riley (better known as Riley Keough) and a son named Benjamin Keough. Unfortunately, Benjamin tragically passed away in July 2020 at the age of 27.

After divorcing Keough in 1994, Lisa Marie had high-profile marriages to Michael Jackson and actor Nicolas Cage, both of which ended in divorce. In 2006, she married musician and producer Michael Lockwood, and they had twin daughters named Harper and Finley before divorcing in 2016.

Lisa Marie Presley's early life and family relationships have been intertwined with fame, music, and personal struggles. Despite the challenges she has faced, she continues to navigate her own path in the music industry and carries on the legacy of her iconic father, Elvis Presley.

1.1 Personal Life and High-Profile Marriages

Lisa Marie Presley's personal life has been marked by a series of high-profile marriages and personal struggles. Here is an overview of her marriages and significant relationships:

1. Danny Keough (1988-1994): Lisa Marie's first marriage was to musician Danny Keough in 1988. They had two children together, a daughter named Danielle Riley (known as Riley Keough) and a son named Benjamin Keough. Despite their eventual divorce in 1994, Danny and Lisa Marie have maintained an amicable relationship, co-parenting their children before her demiss.

2. Michael Jackson (1994-1996): Following her divorce from Danny Keough, Lisa Marie ventures into sphere of marriage again, this time with pop icon Michael Jackson in 1994. Their relationship drew intense media scrutiny due to the combination of two famous families and all eyes were on them. However, their marriage was short-lived and ended in divorce in 1996. Lisa Marie publicly supported Michael during various legal controversies, even after their separation.

3. Nicolas Cage (2002): Lisa Marie's third marriage was to actor Nicolas Cage in 2002, the two love bird met and tied the knot. Their union was unfortunately a very brief one, lasting only a few months before they filed for divorce.

4. Michael Lockwood (2006-2016): Lisa Marie's longest maried again, and this time it was to musician and producer Michael Lockwood. They tied the knot in 2006 and had twin daughters named Harper and Finley in 2008, it was the longest marriage Lisa Marie had in her lifetime, their marriage lasted 10 years. However, the couple faced marital difficulties, leading to their divorce in 2016. And in 2021 their decade marriage ended, though finalized but was shadowed by unresolved issues, which was followed by a highly publicized and contentious legal battle over financial and custody issues.

Beyond her marriages, Lisa Marie has also faced personal struggles and challenges. She has been open about her battles with addiction and has sought treatment for substance abuse. Additionally, Lisa Marie has experienced the profound loss of her son Benjamin Keough, who tragically passed away in July 2020.

Throughout her personal ups and downs, Lisa Marie Presley has demonstrated resilience and a commitment to her family. She continues to navigate the complexities of fame and personal life while striving to maintain a sense of stability and growth for herself and her children.

CHAPTER 2: MOTHERHOOD AND PARENTING JOURNEY OF LISA MARIE PRESLEY

Motherhood has been a significant aspect of Lisa Marie Presley's life and her parenting journey has had its own unique challenges and joys. Here's a glimpse into her experience as a mother:

Lisa Marie has four children, and her journey as a mother has been a central focus of her life. Her eldest children, Danielle Riley (Riley Keough) and Benjamin Keough(late), are from her first marriage to Danny Keough and ahw loved both of them like as a mother would. She also has twin daughters, Harper and Finley, from her marriage to Michael Lockwood.

As a mother, Lisa Marie has strived to provide her children with a sense of stability and love.

She has worked to create a nurturing environment for them, balancing the complexities of fame and their privacy. Despite her own struggles and the legacy of her iconic father, Elvis Presley, Lisa Marie has sought to shield her children from excessive media attention and guide them through the challenges of growing up in the public eye.

Like any parent, Lisa Marie has faced the usual joys and struggles of raising children. She has emphasized the importance of family and maintaining strong bonds. Lisa Marie has also encouraged her children to pursue their own passions and interests, supporting them in their individual endeavors.

Tragically, Lisa Marie experienced the heartbreaking loss of her son, Benjamin Keough, in 2020. The loss of a child is an unimaginable and devastating experience, and it undoubtedly had a profound impact on Lisa

Marie and her family. Dealing with such grief while continuing to navigate the responsibilities of being a mother is an ongoing challenge that she has had to face.

Through it all, Lisa Marie's love for her children and her commitment to their well-being has remained unwavering. She has worked to create a sense of normalcy and a strong foundation for them, nurturing their individuality and supporting their dreams.

While the specifics of Lisa Marie Presley's motherhood journey are largely private, it is evident that her role as a mother has played a significant part in her life, shaping her priorities and influencing her decisions. Like any parent, she has faced both triumphs and challenges, finding strength and resilience along the way.

2.1 Relationship with Elvis Presley, the King of Rock and Roll

Lisa Marie Presley had a unique and significant relationship with her father, Elvis Presley. As the only child of the legendary musician, Lisa Marie held a special place in Elvis's life, and their bond was both loving and complex.

Elvis adored his daughter and was deeply involved in her life, even during the tumultuous period following his divorce from Lisa Marie's mother, Priscilla Presley. Despite their separation, Elvis made sure to spend quality time with Lisa Marie, often taking her on vacations and visits to his Graceland mansion. He cherished their father-daughter moments and showered her with affection and attention.

Lisa Marie's relationship with Elvis was characterized by a strong emotional connection. She was known to be a daddy's girl and was deeply influenced by her father's musical talents and larger-than-life persona. Elvis's passion for music left an indelible mark on Lisa Marie, igniting her own passion for the industry and inspiring her to pursue a career as a singer.

Tragically, Lisa Marie was only nine years old when Elvis passed away in August 1977. His sudden death had a profound impact on her life and shaped her understanding of fame, loss, and her own identity. As the sole heir to Elvis's estate, Lisa Marie inherited his legacy and became the custodian of his music, Graceland, and other memorabilia.

In adulthood, Lisa Marie has been dedicated to preserving her father's memory and musical heritage. She has been actively involved in managing Graceland and has participated in numerous projects to celebrate and honor Elvis's contributions to music. Additionally, she has released music that pays tribute to her father and explores their shared musical roots.

While their time together was cut short, the bond between Lisa Marie Presley and Elvis Presley remains a significant part of their respective legacies. Their relationship, marked by love, admiration, and the shared pursuit of musical passion, continues to resonate with fans and enthusiasts of the Presley family.

CHAPTER 3: LISA MARIE PRESLEY'S MUSIC CAREER AND DISCOGRAPHY

Lisa Marie Presley's music career has been a reflection of her own artistic journey and personal experiences. Influenced by her father's musical legacy, she embarked on her own path as a singer-songwriter, exploring various genres and styles throughout her discography.

In 1997, Lisa Marie signed a recording contract with Capitol Records and released her debut album, "To Whom It May Concern." The album received mixed reviews but managed to achieve moderate commercial success. It showcased Lisa Marie's introspective songwriting style, blending elements of rock, pop, and blues. The lead single, "Lights Out," garnered attention and helped establish her as a musical artist in her own right.

Following her debut, Lisa Marie released her second album, "Now What," in 2005. This album delved into more personal and emotional themes, with Lisa Marie's lyrics reflecting her experiences with love, loss, and self-discovery. Though it didn't achieve widespread commercial success, the album received critical praise for its honesty and vulnerability.

In 2012, Lisa Marie released her third studio album, "Storm & Grace." Produced by acclaimed musician T-Bone Burnett, the album showcased a mature and rootsy sound, drawing influences from Americana and folk-rock. Lisa Marie's introspective songwriting took center stage, with her lyrics delving into themes of redemption, resilience, and personal growth. "Storm & Grace" received positive reviews and marked a stylistic shift in Lisa Marie's musical direction.

Throughout her career, Lisa Marie has continued to explore her musical creativity. She has released singles and collaborations, showcasing her versatility as an artist. Her music often reflects her personal journey, addressing topics such as family, relationships, and her own struggles.

While Lisa Marie Presley's music career may not have reached the same level of commercial success as her father's, she has carved out her own niche in the industry. Her unique blend of genres, introspective songwriting, and her connection to the Presley legacy have garnered her a loyal fan base. Lisa Marie's music continues to evolve, showcasing her growth as an artist and her ongoing exploration of her own artistic identity.

3.1 Lisa Marie Presley's Philanthropic Work and Activism

Lisa Marie Presley has been involved in various philanthropic works and activism throughout her life. She has supported several charitable causes and used her platform to raise awareness about important social issues. Here are some highlights of her philanthropic efforts and activism:

1. Presley Charitable Foundation: In 2003, Lisa Marie established the Presley Charitable Foundation, a nonprofit organization aimed at providing support and funding to charitable organizations. The foundation focuses on causes related to homelessness, children in need, victims of domestic violence, and animal welfare.

2. The Dream Factory: Lisa Marie has been an active supporter of The Dream Factory, an organization that grants the wishes of critically

and chronically ill children. She has participated in fundraising events and donated to the organization to help fulfill the dreams of children facing health challenges.

3. Global AIDS Crisis: Lisa Marie has shown her commitment to raising awareness about the global AIDS crisis. She has supported organizations such as amfAR (The Foundation for AIDS Research) and participated in events to raise funds for HIV/AIDS research and prevention.

4. Children's Hospital Los Angeles: Lisa Marie has been involved with the Children's Hospital Los Angeles, supporting their efforts to provide comprehensive healthcare to children in need. She has made donations and participated in events to benefit the hospital and its young patients.

5. Animal Welfare: Lisa Marie has been an advocate for animal welfare and has supported organizations such as the Best Friends Animal Society, which focuses on rescuing and finding homes for animals in need. She has used her platform to promote animal adoption and raise awareness about the importance of treating animals with compassion and care.

6. Veterans Support: Lisa Marie has shown her support for veterans and military service members. She has been involved with organizations such as the Veterans Village in Las Vegas, which provides housing and support services to homeless veterans. Lisa Marie has participated in fundraising events and awareness campaigns to address the unique challenges faced by veterans.

7. Disaster Relief Efforts: In times of natural disasters, Lisa Marie has stepped up to contribute to relief efforts. She has made donations to organizations working on disaster relief and recovery, helping communities affected by events like hurricanes, earthquakes, and wildfires.

8. Breast Cancer Awareness: Lisa Marie has been an advocate for breast cancer awareness. She has supported organizations like the Susan G. Komen Foundation and has used her platform to encourage women to undergo regular screenings, promote early detection, and raise funds for breast cancer research.

9. LGBTQ+ Rights: Lisa Marie has expressed her support for the LGBTQ+ community and has spoken out against discrimination and inequality. She has participated in events and campaigns promoting LGBTQ+ rights and equality.

10. Arts and Education: Lisa Marie recognizes the importance of arts and education in fostering creativity and personal growth. She has contributed to initiatives that support arts education in schools and has donated to organizations focused on providing educational opportunities to underprivileged children.

11. Mental Health Awareness: Lisa Marie has been vocal about mental health issues and the importance of destigmatizing mental health struggles. She has shared her own experiences and advocated for increased access to mental health resources and support services.

In addition to her philanthropic endeavors, Lisa Marie has also been active in using her voice to bring attention to social issues. She has spoken out about mental health, addiction, and the importance of seeking help and support. Her openness about her personal struggles has helped reduce the stigma surrounding these issues and encouraged others to seek help when needed.

Lisa Marie Presley's philanthropic works and activism reflect her dedication to making a positive impact in the lives of others. Through her charitable efforts and advocacy, she strives to create awareness, support important causes, and inspire others to contribute to the betterment of society.

She has demonstrated a commitment to various causes and has used her platform to make a positive impact in the lives of others.

CHAPTER 4: CHALLENGES AND STRUGGLES IN LISA MARIE PRESLEY'S LIFE

Lisa Marie Presley has faced a number of challenges and struggles throughout her life which has made her to be strong and to stand the test of time. Here are some significant challenges and struggles she encountered and came out with victories:

1. Loss of Loved Ones: Lisa Marie has experienced the tragic loss of several loved ones, which has had a profound impact on her. The most devastating loss was the death of her father, Elvis Presley, when she was only nine years old. This loss not only affected her emotionally but also placed her in the spotlight as the sole heir to Elvis's estate at that young age, with all eyes fixed on her globally. Additionally, Lisa also lost her son unexpectedly Benjamin Keough, in 2020,

which brought immense grief and heartache to Lisa Marie and her family.

2. Media Scrutiny and Public Attention:

Growing up as the daughter of Elvis Presley, Lisa Marie was subjected to intense media scrutiny from a young age. Her personal life and relationships have been constantly under the public eye, often leading to invasive and sensationalized coverage. Managing fame and maintaining privacy has been an ongoing challenge for her.

3. Personal Struggles and Addiction:
Lisa Marie has been candid about her struggles with addiction and mental health. She has faced personal battles with substance abuse, seeking treatment and working towards recovery. Her openness about these challenges has helped reduce stigma and has encouraged others to seek help and support.

4. Relationship Turmoil: Lisa Marie's romantic relationships have faced their fair share of challenges. Her marriages have experienced difficulties and ended in divorce. The breakdown of these relationships has been a source of personal pain and has played out publicly in the media, adding to the emotional strain she has endured.

5. Legal and Financial Issues: Lisa Marie has encountered legal and financial challenges over the years. These include legal disputes, financial mismanagement, and debt. Navigating legal battles and financial setbacks has added additional stress and complexity to her life.

Despite these challenges, Lisa Marie Presley has demonstrated resilience and determination. She has sought support, worked on personal growth, and used her experiences to connect with others facing similar struggles.

Through it all, she continues to navigate her journey, striving to find stability, happiness, and fulfillment in her personal and professional life.

4.1 Lisa Marie Presley's Artistic Ventures Outside of Music

Beyond her music career, Lisa Marie Presley has also explored artistic ventures in various other creative fields. Here are some notable endeavors outside of music:

1. Writing: Lisa Marie has delved into writing and has expressed herself through her words. She published a critically acclaimed autobiography titled "Elvis by the Presleys" in 2005, which provided an intimate look into her life and her perspective on her father, Elvis Presley. The book offered personal insights and reflections from Lisa Marie and other family members.

2. Acting: Lisa Marie has explored acting and appeared in a few film and television projects. In 1988, she made her acting debut in the film "The Adventures of Ford Fairlane" alongside Andrew Dice Clay. She also had a guest

appearance in the television series "Touched by an Angel" in 1998.

3. Visual Arts: Lisa Marie has expressed her creativity through visual arts, including painting. While not widely publicized, she has pursued painting as a form of artistic expression, creating artwork that reflects her emotions and personal experiences.

4. Photography: Lisa Marie has also shown an interest in photography. She has taken photographs and shared them on her social media platforms, offering glimpses into her perspective and capturing moments from her life and travels.

It's worth noting that while Lisa Marie has explored these artistic ventures, her primary focus and recognition have been in the music industry. However, her forays into other artistic fields showcase her multifaceted nature and her desire to express herself through various creative outlets.

CHAPTER 5: LISA MARIE PRESLEY'S CONNECTION TO THE ELVIS PRESLEY ESTATE

Lisa Marie Presley has a significant connection to the Elvis Presley Estate, which encompasses the assets, properties, and legacy associated with her father, Elvis Presley. As the only child of Elvis, Lisa Marie has played a crucial role in preserving and managing her father's estate.

Upon Elvis's passing in 1977, Lisa Marie inherited the majority of her father's estate, including Graceland, his iconic mansion in Memphis, Tennessee. Since then, she has been actively involved in the management and preservation of Graceland, ensuring its continued operation as a museum and a place for Elvis fans to visit and celebrate his life and music.

Lisa Marie has worked diligently to expand and enhance Graceland's offerings, overseeing the development of new exhibits, events, and experiences for visitors. Under her guidance, Graceland has become one of the most popular tourist destinations in the United States, attracting millions of visitors each year.

In addition to managing Graceland, Lisa Marie has also been involved in licensing and merchandising efforts related to her father's image and music. She has worked with partners to ensure that Elvis's legacy is respected and represented in a manner befitting his status as a cultural icon.

However, in recent years, Lisa Marie has faced legal and financial challenges related to her personal life and the management of the Elvis Presley Estate. These challenges have included legal disputes, financial issues, and changes in the estate's ownership structure. As a result, the estate's management has undergone some changes, but Lisa Marie's connection to her father's legacy and her involvement in preserving his memory remain significant aspects of her life.

Overall, Lisa Marie Presley's connection to the Elvis Presley Estate has allowed her to carry on her father's musical legacy, manage his assets, and ensure that his impact on popular culture endures for future generations.

5.1 Lisa Marie Presley's Legacy and Impact on Pop Culture

The legacy of Lisa Marie Presley's father, Elvis Presley, has had an enduring impact on pop culture, and Lisa Marie herself has contributed to that legacy in various ways. Here are some aspects of the Presley family's impact on pop culture:

1. Elvis Presley's Musical Influence: Elvis Presley is often referred to as the "King of Rock and Roll" and is one of the most influential figures in the history of popular music. His fusion of various genres, including rock, country, gospel, and rhythm and blues, created a new sound that revolutionized the music industry. Elvis's energetic performances, unique style, and charismatic stage presence helped shape the landscape of popular music and inspired countless artists who followed. Lisa Marie, as his daughter, carries on his musical legacy through her own music career

and serves as a connection between Elvis's iconic status and contemporary music.

2. Graceland and Elvis Tourism: Graceland, Elvis Presley's mansion in Memphis, Tennessee, has become a symbol of his legacy and a pilgrimage site for fans from around the world. Lisa Marie's involvement in the management and development of Graceland has helped preserve its historical and cultural significance. The estate offers guided tours, exhibits, and events, allowing fans to immerse themselves in Elvis's life and music. Graceland's popularity as a tourist attraction has had a significant impact on Memphis's economy and solidified Elvis's status as an enduring cultural icon.

3. Preserving Elvis's Image: Lisa Marie has played a vital role in preserving and protecting her father's image and brand. She has been involved in licensing and merchandising efforts

to ensure that Elvis's image is used appropriately and in accordance with his legacy. This has allowed Elvis's image to remain visible in popular culture through various merchandise, documentaries, tribute concerts, and other forms of media.

4. Cultural Icon Status: Elvis Presley's impact on popular culture extends beyond his music. His rebellious image, distinctive fashion choices, and cultural impact made him an icon of his era. Elvis's influence can be seen in the evolution of popular music, fashion trends, and even societal attitudes. His legacy continues to be celebrated and referenced in films, television shows, and music, with his name and image recognized worldwide.

5. Performers who impersonate and pay tribute to Elvis Presley: Elvis's enduring popularity has led to the emergence of countless Elvis impersonators and tribute

artists, who pay homage to his music, style, and stage presence. These performers keep the spirit of Elvis alive and contribute to the ongoing fascination with his legacy. Lisa Marie's presence and involvement in the Elvis tribute community serve as a link between the fans and the Presley family.

Lisa Marie Presley, as the daughter of Elvis Presley, has been an integral part of the ongoing impact and legacy of the Presley family in pop culture. Through her own endeavors and her dedication to preserving her father's memory, she ensures that Elvis's influence continues to resonate with audiences worldwide.

Conclusion

In summary, The Life and Times of Lisa Marie Presley is one which reveals the exceptional journey through the highs and lows, triumphs and challenges, showcasing the unyielding spirit of a woman who stepped out from the shadow of a legend to create her own path. Delving into the intricacies of Lisa Marie's multifaceted personality, its an avenue to uncovers her layers of vulnerability, strength, and resilience.

From her early years as Elvis Presley's daughter to her ascent to fame and the personal struggles she encountered, unbreakable provides a profound exploration of Lisa Marie's life. It exposes the profound influence her father had on her identity and the choices she made to establish herself as an individual. Through intimate insights and thorough research, the biography reveals the personal triumphs and heartaches that shaped her journey.

As the guardian of the Elvis Presley legacy, Lisa Marie's unwavering commitment to preserving her father's memory shines through the pages of this biography. Her dedication to honoring his legacy while making her own lasting impact on the world exemplifies her strength and determination. Navigating fame, personal challenges, and the weight of immense expectations, she faced it all with unwavering courage.

"Unbreakable" offers a rare peek into private moments and untold stories behind the public persona, highlighting Lisa Marie's resilience in the face of adversity and her relentless pursuit of self-discovery. Throughout, she remained unbreakable, overcoming life's challenges and leaving an indelible mark on the world.

This biography serves as a reminder that beyond fame and name, there is a person with hopes, dreams, and struggles. Lisa Marie Presley's journey embodies strength, resilience, and the unwavering spirit of a woman who forged her own path and emerged as a formidable force.

"Unbreakable: The Life and Times of Lisa Marie Presley" stands as a testament to the power of perseverance, the intricacies of fame, and the enduring legacy of a woman firmly established in popular culture. It encourages readers to recognize the depth of her story and the indomitable spirit within her.

CAUSE OF DEATH

On Thursday January 12, 2023, it was confirmed by experts the passing of Lisa Marie Presley at age 54, attributing her demise to complications arising from an extensive bariatric procedure.

The Los Angeles District Clinical Inspector Coroner's office released an examination report on the eve of that day, providing additional details about the circumstances surrounding Lisa's death.

According to the report, filed by the inspector, Presley's complications were typical for bariatric surgery, which is a weight reduction method that is often done when other strategies of losing weight fail, prove ineffective or in the presence of a severe illness.

Lisa Marie Presley breathed her last at a Los Angeles hospital, where paramedics, responding to a cardiac arrest emergency call at her home, on the way to west hills hospital in Los Angeles, the team of paramedics tried to revive her heart by administering CPR before she was rushed for treatment. After her death, an autopsy was done to detect the cause of her death, but no immediate indications of the underlying cause was revealed.

Earlier in the day, she had complained of a serious abdominal pain, as noted in the post-mortem report.

Her final resting place was at a memorial service held at Graceland on Jan. 22, the iconic home where she spent her childhood, now transformed into a museum, tourist attraction, and sanctuary for Elvis enthusiasts.

Riley Keough, the daughter of Lisa Marie Presley, now 34-years old, who is an actress from "Daisy Jones and the Six," and Harper and Finley Lockwood, 15-year-old twins, were the three daughters left by Lisa Marie Presley. Her only son Benjamin Keough, a child, passed away before her death in 2020.

In the immediate aftermath of Presley's demise, there were indications of a potential legal dispute over her estate. Priscilla Presley, their grandmother, filed court papers challenging a 2016 amendment to Lisa Marie Presley's living trust, replacing her and a former business manager as legal administrators with her two eldest children just four days after the funeral.

However, in May, 2023, Priscilla Presley and Riley Keough, who now serves as the sole trustee, reached an agreement.This was done in L.A by superior judge Lynn H scaduto On Wednesday. It was officially documented that Riley keough the granddaughter of priscilla and Elvis Presley as the sole trustee of Lisa Marie trust, this new development made pricilia to resign as co trustee in exchange for other benefits and compensation.

Riley Keough received her first Emmy nomination for her role in "Daisy Jones & the Six" as the best actress in a limited series or TV movie. And she's moving to take on the presley's legacy to greater heights.

Made in the USA
Monee, IL
11 August 2024